# Woodworking:

## Top 40 DIY Woodworking Projects With Step-by-Step Instructions (Building Cabinets, Bookcases & Shelves)

# Table of Contents

* * * * * * * * * * * * * * * * * * * * * * * * * * * * * * * * * * * * * * * * * * * * * * * * * * * *

## Introduction: Know Your Tools

Before we delve right into the projects I wanted to elaborate a bit further on the types of wood working tools that you will be using. In this chapter here is a brief rundown of some of the most important.

***Power Drill***

This standard wood working tool is extremely important since it is the main means of stitching your wood working together.

***Tape Measure***

This one is probably more or less common sense, but when you need to make measurements, as you do in wood working, having an accurate tape measure is a must!

***Jigsaw***

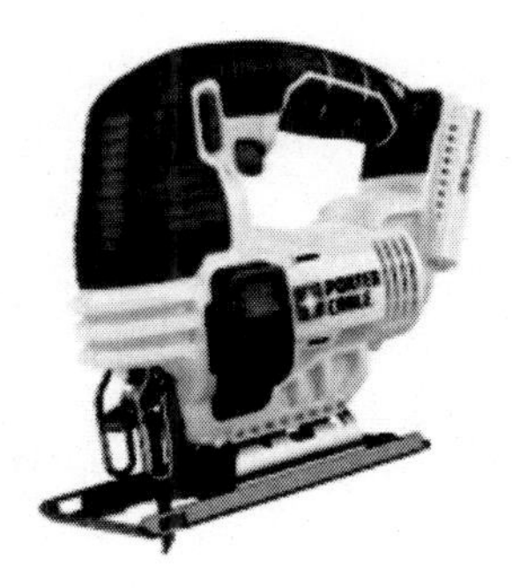

The jigsaw is used to cut curves and works out great for circular tables and other surfaces that need just a little more detail.

***Hand Saw***

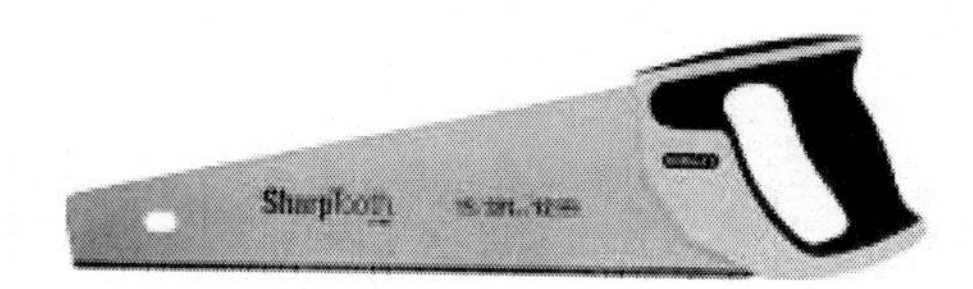

Hand saws are instrumental in cutting through your would, and most importantly they are instrumental in cross-cutting, and smoothing out any rough edges. This tool is absolutely critical when it comes to fashioning your wood down to its ultimate dimensions, so be sure to have one on hand.

***Power Jointer***

This tool is fundamental in straightening out edges, and probably flattens down rough and rugged wood better than any other tool you could use. This tool is a prepping tool more than anything else, and is of great advantage when you are just starting to build your wood working project.

# Chapter 1: Living Room Furnishings

The living room is where we try to relax, and our living room fixtures and furnishings need to reflect that fact. Here in this chapter learn to create a whole new living room décor with the great pieces of DIY wood working furniture presented here.

## ***Wooden Sleeve Couch Cup Holder***

This one is pretty basic. All you really have to do is take 1 wooden 2 by 4 and cut it into three equal pieces. You are then going to want to take out your power jointer and use it to smooth out the rough edges of the board. After you have done this, lay one of the pieces flat and take another piece and stand it up on its side, and place it right next to the piece that is laying flat. Nail this piece to the side of the board that is laying flat.

Now take our other piece of wood and nail it to the opposite side of the flat board. With the assembly complete flip the frame over to where it is standing up. Take a cup out from your cupboard and put it down in the center of your top board. Now take a black magic marker and trace a circle around the cup. Now take out your jigsaw and use it to carve out the circle you have just traced. Now just pop this wooden sleeve up on the arm of your couch and put your favorite drink to rest in its cup holder!

***Junk Box***

We all have extra junk that needs to be put somewhere, so lets make a box completely devoted to the enterprise! To get started, take out a 2 by 4 of wood and cut it evenly in half. Now put these halves together—either with woodworking glue, or by nailing them. This will serve as the bottom of your box. Once your bottom is in place you can then work on the walls. Fashion out corresponding walls to match your box's bottom and seal them in place with wood working glue. Just let your glue dry and your junk box is complete!

***Wooden Doormat***

First measure out your wood with your tape measurer and mark the measurements with pencil, before cutting them out. The end result should yield you several 16 by 18 balusters. After this, take out your power drill and with a 3 by 8 drill bit, create holes at each end of your boards. Use your power jointer to smooth out any rough edges then get some good wood stain and stain your pieces of wood. Now simply glue these pieces of wood together and your wooden doormat is ready for use.

***Pipe Table***

First your pipe needs to be cut to length and threaded. Fortunately, if you don't have the equipment yourself, many home improvement stores such as Lowes and Home Depot will be more than happy to do it for you. Your pipes need to be ¾ of an inch in diameter and 6 inches long, eight pipes in total. Now simply attach your pipes together to create a working framework for your table. Now attach a large slab of fresh wood to the frame and your pipe table is finished.

***Rustic Spoon Hook Hangers***

This woodworking DIY adds some real flair to your living room. And all you nee to make it is one 2 x 4 piece of wood and 8 spoons. First take the 2 x 4 and sand it down, making sure to remove imperfections. Next, take your spoons and drill them (spoon side) right into the mid section of the wood, spacing each spoon evenly apart. Now simply bend each spoon handle upward into a hook. Put this Rustic Spoon Hook Hanger up on the wall and its ready to go.

***Piano Bench***

Even if you don't play the piano, this piano bench could be a stylish addition to your living room décor. To get started you need to choose the kind of wood that you feel best matches your piano and (or) your other living room furnishings.

Just to give you an idea, most piano benches are constructed from mahogany, maple, and ebony wood materials.

Next you need to measure out your materials. First you are going to put the bottom frame together by taking a 29 by 1 inch piece of wood and setting it down on a flat work area. Now take out two pieces measuring 27 by 1 inch and set them down on each side of this bottom frame, these will comprise the main leg support. Next, two 12 by 1 inch pieces of wood and attach them to these legs, gluing everything in place. You now have a working piano bench.

***Small Stool/Stand***

This stool consists of 9 basic parts. The seat, four legs, and four brace boards. First fashion out four 8 inch long legs for your stool, then create four 3 inch long brace boards, along with your 4 by 6 inch seat. First nail your brace boards to your legs, and then attach your seat with either wood working glue or screws. Your small stool/stand is complete.

***Murphy Desk***

This desk is convenient and saves on space since it is attached directly to the wall. Just get out a flat board approximately 6 by 14 inches ad nail it to your wall. This is the main backing support structure. Follow this by taking a board that is of the same exact size and nailing it right in the mid-center of the board you nailed on the wall. Your Murphy Desk is now ready for business.

***Shoe Rack***

This shoe rack is another great space saver and fairly easy to construct. You will need five 2 by 2 planks and four 2 by 4's. Evenly space out your 2 by 2 boards and then stabilize them by nailing a 2 by 4 in each corner. After you have done this your shoe rack is finished.

## Chapter 2: Kitchen Cabinets

The kitchen isn't just a place to eat and cook; it should be a place of comfort and warm familiarity with a bit of pizzazz! Here are some DIY wood working projects that can do just that!

***Giant Wooden Silverware***

I remember these from when I was a kid; my grandma had one of the classic giant wooden spoon and fork hanging from her wall. I used to imagine that this was the silver wear that the giant from Jack and Bean Stalk used to eat his food! But you don't need to be a giant in order to enjoy this fine piece of wood work. You just need some wood and a basic handsaw.

To get stared, simply take out a large piece of plywood and put it to the side. Now take a black magic marker and draw the dimensions of your spoon and fork right on the board. Pick up your hand saw and start cutting right along the magic marker lines you have drawn until your spoon and fork are completely cut out of the wood. You now have the silverware of giants.

***Napkin Holder***

This fun little woodworking DIY can add a lot of charm to your kitchen, and since it is such a small craft to construct, it doesn't take much wood. In fact, all you are going to need is a 2 by 6 inch block of wood as a base and two 1 by 5 inch panels of wood for the walls of the holder. You can either leave these as plain blocks, or you can carve a design such as the one depicted above. Just glue the assembly in place and your napkin holder is complete.

***Wooden Bottle Opener***

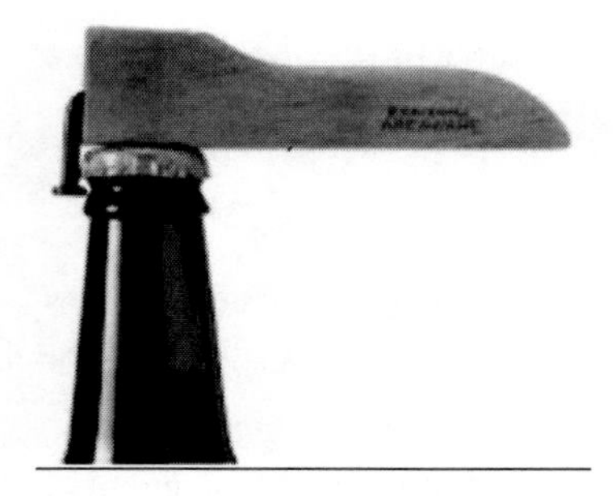

This is a woodworking DIY that can serve a purpose! It is easy yet ingenious to construct. Just carve a 3 inch long piece of wood out of a board, and carve a gentle curve on its back to serve as its handle. Next, hammer a nail into the front of the block and bend it all the way forward to where it is hanging over the edge of the wood. Now to open your select beverage of choice, simply press the wood block to the cap of the bottle and hook the extended nail underneath the bottle cap. Just pull up an putting pressure on the wooden handle with your hand and the bottle cap will pop right up. You can have a drink to celebrate this wood working DIY!

***Wooden Cutting Board***

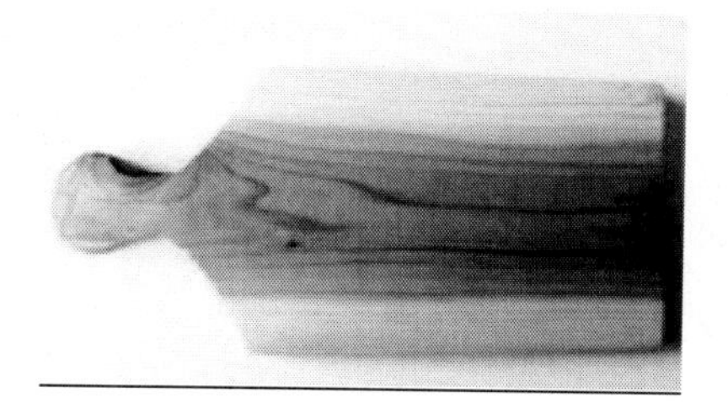

Cutting boards are great; they are simple yet serve a purpose. I personally don't know where my sub sandwiches would be without them! Where would I chop all those veggies and meats for my midnight snack? Anyway! In order to create your own wooden cutting board, carve a 4 inch by 8 inch rectangle out of a block of wood about an inch and a half thick. After you have done this take your jigsaw to carve the curves on top of the board that will create your handle. Your board is now ready for some serious cutting action.

***Basic Utility Cabinet***

These durable utility cabinets are great for extra items that might be hanging out in the kitchen. All you need to construct this cabinet is three medium sized pieces of plywood shelving and 5 2 x 4's used to brace the structure. Lay out your plywood shelves, standing on their sides on a flat surface, and then attach a 2 x 4 to each end cap facing you. After securing this, simply turn your assembly over and then take two more of your 2 x 4's and affix them to the end caps on the other side. Finally, take your remaining 2 x 4 and fasten it right in the middle of the assembly. Your basic utility cabinet is now ready for use.

***<u>Paneled Cabinet Doors</u>***

Sometimes just by putting a new set of covering for the doors on your cabinet you can give our whole kitchen a face lift. Just take your plywood paneling and affix it to your cabinet doors with strong wood working glue. Now just add a layer of wood staining to the cabinet and your newly paneled cabinet doors will be in great shape.

***Wall Cabinet***

These wall cabinets are convenient for your kitchen items, and they also add an extra level of class to your overall kitchen setup. To g started take out a large, 2 inch thick section of plywood and sketch out your cabinet's dimensions. Use a black magic marker to draw the door, top, bottom, walls, backing and shelves. Cut out these specified dimensions and then set your backing piece on a flat surface.

From this base you can then glue on your top, bottom, and walls. Now insert your shelving into the cabinet. You can create as many shelves as you think appropriate but usually just three or four should suffice. Now pick up your door piece and drill a pair of high quality brass hinges to the door, and then attach these hinges to your left side cabinet wall, thereby installing your door and completing your cabinet. This wall cabinet can now be nailed to the wall of your kitchen.

***Gun Cabinet***

Similar to a standard bookcase, the main difference here it he door to the cabinet itself. The main wood frame should be ¾ of an inch thick and the smaller partitions should be ½ of an inch thick. The doors should be put in place right inside the cabinet, with door frames holding them in place by special molding. These doors should be made to fit the sides and should reach over the edge. And that's it! Just load up your cabinet!

***Magnetic Knife Strip***

In order to create a magnetic knife strip you will need a medium sized piece of wood about 1 inch thick. Next take your power drill and drill out an in inch slot in the middle of the wood. Insert your magnetic strip here. Your knives should now be attracted, and stick to the wood. Hang this up right on your wall and your kitchen will be all the more stylish for it.

## Chapter 3: Bedroom Shelves, Bookcases, and More

The bedroom is the most personal part of the home, it is where you sleep, but it is also where you share your most intimate thoughts and moments. With that in mind, this chapter sets to recreate those moments in wood!

***Study Table***

This is a nifty little table for your bedroom. To get started cut out a medium sized piece of plywood for your table top, into a perfect square. Next cut out four legs that are 2 feet long and 4 inches wide, as well as 2 inches thick. Attach these legs to your table top and your study table is finished.

***Wooden Horseshoe Candle Holder***

This one is pretty simple. Just take one 2 x4 piece of wood and cut it in half. Now take one of the halves and measure out five even spaces for where your candles will be. Now use your jigsaw to cut out five circles of the same exact size. This is where your candles will be inserted. Finally, nail a horseshow to each end, making sure that the tops of the horseshoes are level with the top of the board. You can now stand up this classy candle holder right on your nightstand, bookcase, or shelf.

***Desk Rack***

To get started on this one, just flesh out the recommended dimensions and begin gluing! That's really all there is to it! Now just find a good place to put it! Enjoy your Desk Rack!

***X-Shaped Night Stand***

Night stands are convenient; this is where you put your water when you wake up at 1 in the morning with a dry mouth! Having that said, this piece of furniture is important, so you need to get it right. Start off by creating your box, this can be done by taking a medium sized board for the base of the box, next, take four 2 foot long boards and nail them up as your walls. Now take a medium board more or less identical to the bottom one and nail it on top.

With this assembly in place you can then move on to constructing the legs. You will need four legs of course, and they should all be a foot and a half in length. Once your legs are carved out cross them in pairs, right in the middle. Now nail the tops of your legs to the box. Now you need to create a cross section that reaches from the front legs to the back. Your X-Shaped Night Stand is now complete.

***Bed And Breakfast Table***

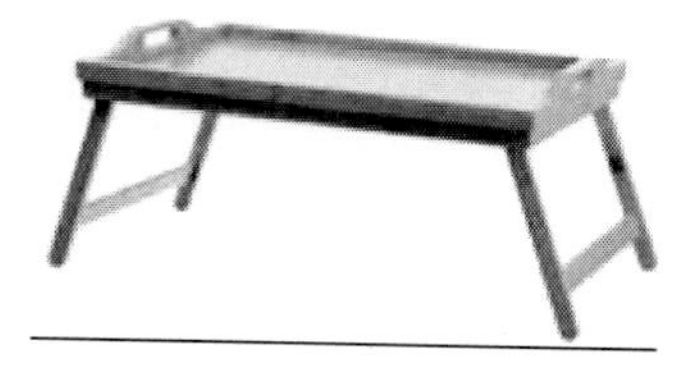

If you would like to surprise your significant other with Breakfast in Bed and Breakfast Tables are perfect for the task. Start off by getting a board that is 8 feet long, 2 feet wide and an inch and a half thick. Next construct your legs by cutting out wooden beams that are 4 feet long, 2 inches wide and 1 inch thick. Attach the tops of the legs to the 8 foot board. And as simple as that, your Bed and Breakfast Table is ready to go!

***Wooden Bookends***

There is really nothing at all complex about this wood working DIY but that doesn't take the value away from it. It adds a neat touch to your bedroom decorum, to have all of those great book titles of yours held in place between to wooden bookends. The easiest way to create these bookends is to saw off about 2 feet from a 2 x 4. Now cut this piece further in half, rendering to blocks of wood that are the same size. Now take out some sandpaper and use t to smooth out the wood. Now just put some books in between and these Wooden Bookends are done.

***Clothes Rack***

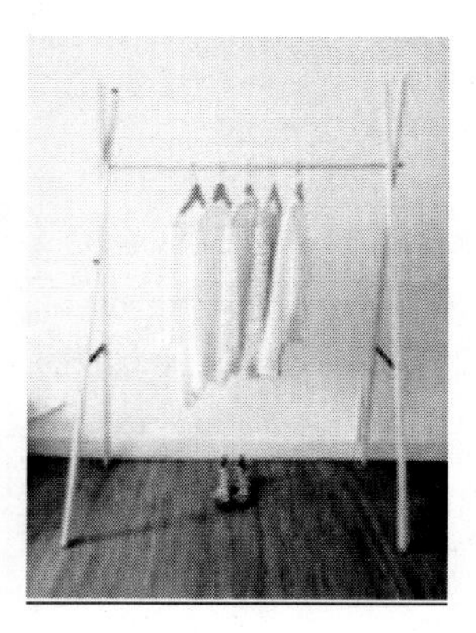

It's always good to have extra closet space, and this highly mobile clothes rack takes the clothes right out of the closet and into the open to give you just that! Construct this one by fashioning out four 6 foot long boards that are 1 and a half inch wide and about an inch thick. Next, fashion out a cross beam that is 3 feet long, one and a half inch wide, and an inch thick, and set it to the side.

Now cross each pair of your long boards at the top and slide your crossbeam right over it, and nail it in place. Next cut out a couple of side stretchers about 3 inches long, and 1 inch wide and nail it to the bottom sides of the long boards, further securing them in place. Now stand the assembly up, place it where you like and you can start hanging your clothes up on your DIY wood worked Clothes Rack.

***Circle Wood Shelf***

---

This is a pretty stylish kind of shelving and looks good just about anywhere. For this one you are going to have to rely heavily on your jigsaw, cutting it in a direct circle. Once your circle is cut out, cut a corresponding board that can fit in the center or a little bit off center in the circle. Now just hang this Circle Wood Shelf up on the wall and you can place whatever decorative items you wish inside of the stylish confines of this Circle Wood Shelf.

***Headboard and Bed Frame***

---

A Headboard and Bed Frame could be constructed out of anything, but for our project we are going to use one of the best wood making materials known to man; pallet boards! And we are not going to use just one pallet board, we are going to use 3 of them! Basically all you have to do is put two of the pallet boards together long ways, nail them together.

Now take the remaining pallet board and stand it up at the head of the two conjoined pallet boards and nail them down on top of the end pallet board. Once this assembly s constructed just make sure that you use your sandpaper to smooth out any rough edges. After that your Headboard and Bed Frame is ready for use.

***Utility Shelves***

These utility shelves are a great fixture in the corner of your bedroom for miscellaneous odds and ends. From a large piece of plywood cut out your shelves, making them a foot and a half long, 3 inches wide, and one inch thick. Now cut out your long boards, making four of them, about 4 feet long each, and 2 inches wide. Finally attach the long boards to the front and back of the shelves and this woodworking DIY is complete.

***Hanging Book Shelf***

For this project you will need some wood stock that is at least half of an inch thick. And the shelf itself should not exceed 2 feet in length. Carefully mark your lines, and cut out your dimensions. Now just put your assembly together and hammer your nails in place. This finished assembly now just needs to be hung up on your wall and your Hanging Book Shelf is complete!

***Corner Shelves***

Your corner shelf should be made to fit the dimensions of your corner, this may vary, but one solid rule to stand by is keeping the wood you use about half an inch thick. First put in your roof, then your walls, and follow this up by nailing your floor in place. Now you can glue in your shelving, finishing up this great wood working project in record time!

***Simple Book Rack***

Here is another wood working project created through a pallet board. All you have to do is cut off the end cap of the pallet board, sand it down with sandpaper and then nail it up on your wall. You can now put all of your favorite books inside this stylish yet Simple Book Rack.

***Photo Ledge***

We all have memories and photos that we cherish. These precious sentimental items need a good place to keep them. This DIY photo ledge can serve as that good place. Start off this wood working project by fashioning two 3 foot long, 2 inch wide, and 2 inch thick boards. Now simple stand these boards together in a "L" shape formation, and either glue or nail them in place. Once this assembly is finished, just nail it up on your wall and put all those great photo memories up on the Photo Ledge.

***Phi Wall Art***

Wall art such as this serves to greatly liven up an otherwise bland exterior. Take a piece of plywood and cut off several 8 inch long, 1 inch thick pieces of wood. Arrange these pieces of wood on your wall in various shapes and designs. Get as creative as you like with this Phi Wall Art.

***Cubby Shelf***

Don't you remember those adorable little cubby holes you had in elementary school? Well, you can upgrade one for your adult self as well. With this wood working DIY you can have a cubby shelf to place all of the important items that your teacher *didn't* take away from you! To get started simply take out a 2 x 4 piece of wood and cut it into 3 inch long, 3 inch wide, and 1 inch thick sections. Now take out another 2 x 4 and repeat this process again. You should now have enough sections to begin construction of your cubby hole. Just stack your squares until the section is complete and repeat.

***Wooden Wardrobe***

This is what just about all of us can use; some extra space for our wardrobe! This DIY makes organization of your clothes an easy task with its streamlined features. In all, for this project you will need 8 wooden pieces that are 195mm x 19mm x 75 mm, 11 wooden pieces that are 175mm x 19mm x 38mm, 10 wooden pieces that are 25mm x 19mm x 38mm, and 4 pieces that are 50mm x 25mm x 75mm respectively.

So get out your hand saw and start cutting out these measurements from your wood. With your pieces fleshed out like the parts of a giant jigsaw puzzle, lay them all flat on the floor. Now put the frame together with your long boards and bottom and top support boards. Next add your shelving and hanging rack. Your Wooden Wardrobe is ready for use.

## Chapter 4: And a Few Easy Extras!

Here are a few miscellaneous extras that you can construct. These wooden DIY's are not necessarily meant for any specific part of the house, feel free to put them anywhere. And have fun!

***Jelly Bean Dispenser***

This is a pretty fun little wood working DIY if I do say so myself! In order to construct this one you will need 12 pieces of wood that are each the exact same dimensions. They should each be 6 inches long, 2 inches wide and 2 inches thick. Take four of these and line them up side by side into a perfect square, with glue in between each piece of wood to hold them together.

Repeat this again with another four pieces, and again the exact same way with the last four pieces. Now stack these four squares together, attaching them with your wood working glue. Next drill a small hole in the center of the square assembly and then drill through the front of the top square until your two drilled holes connect and form a tunnel in which your jelly bean can fall from.

And speaking of jelly beans, fill up a ball jar with the candy, drill a small hole through the lid, put the lid in place, put some glue on the outside of the lid, and quickly flip the jar over on top of the square platform over the hole in the center. Your Jelly Bea dispenser is now ready for service.

***Block Wood Planter***

This one is pretty self explanatory. All you have to do is cut out 2 side boards that are 3 inches long and 2 inches wide (about half an inch thick) and then cut out your end boards making them perfect squares that are 3 inches all the way around (and again about an inch thick). Just glue these boards together and you have yourself a Block Wood Planter!

***Hand Crafted Wooden Picture Frame***

To get this wooden DIY rolling just cut four pieces of wood with the following dimensions; 2 feet long 2 inches wide, and half an inch thick. Once these are fleshed out attach them by slipping two vertical boards underneath the horizontal boards and nail them in place at the corners. You can now add some pictures to your Hand Crafted Wooden Picture Frame.

***Rustic Wooden Pencil Holder***

I get tired of losing all my pencils all the time! Well, guess what? Here is an easy way around that! Here is the Rustic Wooden Pencil Holder! It's really easy to make too! Just cut off the end piece of a 4 x 4 piece of wood and then drill several holes in the top of it. And there you go! An excellent place to put your pencils!

***Decorative Tiny Houses***

I used to have a friend that collected these Decorative Tiny Houses; they are quite popular in many places. And with this DIY you can create your own! Just cut off the last 5 inches or so from a 2 by 4 and then use your hand saw to carve the end of the block you just cut into a point, creating the iconic tiny house shape. Now it's up to you! Be creative and paint and decorate your fantastically Decorative Tiny Houses!

## Conclusion: A Bit of Woodworking Magic!

Woodworking is always an enriching experience, the fact that you can create something out of nothing—out of just a pile of wood—makes it seem somewhat magical. It is this pure and free creative process that keeps me coming back for me. And I hope that you too, have learned how to create your own bit of woodworking magic! Thanks for reading!

**FREE Bonus Reminder**

If you have not grabbed it yet, please go ahead and download your special bonus report *"DIY Projects. 13 Useful & Easy To Make DIY Projects To Save Money & Improve Your Home!"*

Simply Click the Button Below

OR **Go to This Page**

**http://diyhomecraft.com/free**

## BONUS #2: More Free & Discounted Books or Products

**Do you want to receive more Free/Discounted Books or Products?**

We have a mailing list where we send out our new Books or Products when they go free or with a discount on Amazon. Click on the link below to sign up for Free & Discount Book & Product Promotions.

**=> Sign Up for Free & Discount Book & Product Promotions <=**

OR Go to this URL

**http://zbit.ly/1WBb1Ek**

Manufactured by Amazon.ca
Acheson, AB